'BEING ME

Written by

Rachael Thomas

Illustrated by Hannah Browne

S☀CCIONES

Illustrations by Hannah Browne

ISBN: 9798468871836

Typesetting by Socciones Editoria Digitale
www.socciones.co.uk

Miss Sweetie Pie

Rosie Sweetie Pie was her name.
Her job was to sit and smile.
She laughed at jokes and twirled her hair.
That was great, for a while...

Rosie Sweetie Pie lived day to day,
Like every other girl.
She sang and skipped and danced,
Like every other girl.

'Like every other girl,' she thought,
In her pretty, little head.
She looked in the mirror and tilted her gaze.
She slumped down on her pink bed.

"I don't want to be like everyone else."
"This is great, but not quite me."
She shrugged it off as just a phase,
And continued to just be.

She lived day to day like every other girl,
She laughed and skipped like every other girl.

But this time less joyful and with much less spirit.
She knew she was lying; she couldn't run from it.

"What do you want Miss Sweetie Pie?"
"What makes you really smile?"
She looked again, this time harder.
And stayed there for a while

I want to scream and shout and jump,
I want to have that chance.
Play football, cricket, start a fight!
I no longer want to dance.

Girls can't do that, they'll say to me,
And I'll start a strong debate.
This girl can! I'll say right back,
For I'm finally awake.

Do This Do That

Do this, do that.
Sit still.
Be quiet!
I don't know what to do.

What's this, what's that?
Not now.
Line up!
I don't know what to do.

Stop this, stop that.
Stand up.
Hands down!
I don't know what to do.

Do this, do that!
What's this, what's that?
Stop this, stop that.
Can I have some help please?

HARRIET JANE

Miss Harriet Jane was a true British rose.
Perfect plump lips and a cute little nose.
Her hair was blonde and down to her bum.
Long silky legs and a flat iron tum.

She would walk through the streets, and everyone would stare.
"That's Harriet Jane, look over there."
She would look in the mirror and say to herself,
"You're pretty Miss Jane, I adore myself."

Miss Harriet Jane was truly a stunner.
Her eyes were blue like the sea in the summer.
A beautiful creature, anything but plain.
All longed to be Miss Harriet Jane.

The beautiful rose didn't have one friend.
No one to call, no one to depend.
No day of the week or a month in each season.
She's all alone, and here is the reason...

She hasn't a friend, not one to confide.
The beautiful rose, she is ugly inside.
People admire, but only from afar.
Her smile will entice but her bite, it will scar.

Do nice things and be kind to others.
Support one another, sisters, and brothers.
A warm heart is the key, there is no doubt.
If you're ugly inside, your ugly comes out.

Beauty is common, kind-hearted is rare.
Stay humble and thankful for people who care.
Show courage and honesty and most of all passion.
Those are the things, forever in fashion.

As Miss Jane gets older, her name is forgotten.
Her face still shines but her heart is rotten.
She now sits alone each and every meal.
For what stays in mind, is how you make people feel.

Wobbly

There's a wobbly in my tummy.
There's no reason as to why.
There's a wobbly in my tummy.
It makes me want to cry.

There's a wobbly in my tummy.
It can make me act unkind.
There's a wobbly in my tummy.
It makes me hate my mind.

There's a wobbly in my tummy.
My voice warns me in my head.
There's a wobbly in my tummy.
Crawl back into bed.

It used to make me feel frightened.
And a little bit sweaty.
I used to feel this way.
Until I met Miss Betty.

Miss Betty told me that I'm safe.
It's okay to feel this feeling.
I still don't always feel my best.
But I help myself with healing.

I take a deep breath and count to ten.
This seems to do the trick.
My wobbly returns sometimes.
I have a bit a chocolate.

I tell myself, it's okay.
To worry sometimes and feel small.
But pick yourself up and start your day.
Lift your head, stand tall.

There's a wobbly in my tummy.
My heart can start to race.
There's a wobbly in my tummy.
It's something I have to face.

There's a wobbly in my tummy.
And sometimes I need my mam.
There's a wobbly in my tummy.
But I'm okay with who I am.

Just, Stop It!

I'm not okay with the litter on the street.
I'm not okay with dropping litter at your feet.
Adults even do it; you'd think that they'd be smarter.
Just use the bin that's next to you, is that really much harder?
There's plastic in our oceans, get that in your head.
The fish are being trapped and the turtles will be dead.
Your actions are affecting children; the planet they inherit.
Put your litter in the bin, before we all regret it.
Forests are being cut down; we leave nothing but a bruise.
When Santa checks his Christmas lists, how much paper does he use?
We could live so beautifully, oh the world we could have had.
Just put the cardboard in the recycle bin! It makes me really mad.
The bad guy will throw the litter, when will the good guy win?
If you're mad too, say it loud! Put your litter in the bin!

Martha

Martha the duck is very unique.
She was born without wings at all.
She has two flat feet,
A beautiful beak.
But no wings to help her stand tall.

Martha got up every morning.
She would swim to the lake with the wheat.
The other ducks would stare,
But she didn't care.
Just swam along with her flat feet.

Martha didn't have many friends.
All alone every day and all night.
She would look up to the sky,
And ask herself why,
She was the only one without any flight.

There's no shame in asking for help.
This is something that, Martha, she knew.

She went to the black bird.
"Can you help me?" He heard.
Without hesitation, he flew.

Disheartened and pretty downtrodden.
Martha would try again harder.
She said to flamingos,
"Let's go where the cloud goes."
They sneered and wouldn't regard her.

Martha's dream was to glide through the air.
But everyone was mean.
Everyone said nope.
She began to lose hope.
Then Monkey came out of the evergreen.

"Climb on my back, Martha," said Monkey.
"Come with me through the air.
It's just me and you.
Let's make dreams come true.
I can't fly but I'm here and I care."

Martha felt hopeful, trusting him truly.

"I'll climb on your back, hold me tight."
Up trees he climbed.
Across branches and vines.
Soon enough, they would take flight.

Martha felt the wind through her feathers.
The thrill felt empowering to her.
"I'm finally free!"
A leap to each tree.
She was flying without any care.

Martha had imagined flying, different.
A smile across both of their faces.
"It's just you and me.
Across tree to tree.
A found friendship in unlikely of places."

A Day in a Life

I stretch up from my sleep reluctantly.

I eat my eggs politely.

I skip to school joyfully.

I creep through the corridor quietly.

I listen to our learning attentively.

I manage my maths magnificently.

I participate in play time loudly.

I struggle with science sullenly.

I scrounge on my snack furiously.

I sit at my station readily.

I start my stroll home happily.

Repeat routine tomorrow.

TOXIC TOAD

There once was a toxic toad,
Who once said he thought he could sing,
He was strong and tough,
And hairy with fluff,
He considered himself the king.

The gentle frog was kind,
He would never be seen with a frown,
He looked up to the toad,
In his sports car he road,
He considered himself the clown.

The clown and the king they were,
To parties and bars, they would trundle,
The toad he would say, "This party, I slay,"
And take all of the frogs to his puddle.

Queen toad was beautiful,
She shone inside and out,
She was clever and smart, a creator of art.

The most desired creature about.
The gentle frog was considered ugly,
but the queen, she recognised talent,
She said, "It's not the skin, but the beauty within,
He is thoughtful and gentle and gallant."

The toad was angry with rage,
But the queen, she would let him have it,
To be a true king, one does not sing,
But he cares for his people and planet.

WHAT'S YOUR FAVOURITE ANIMAL?

"Elephant!", "Tiger!", "Shark!" and "Cheetah!"
They said to the question asked,
"What is your favourite animal?" he said,
(The new teacher of our class).

"What about you Liam?" he asked again,
As the class turned their head.
"Bees, Sir," I whispered, whilst looking away.
I felt my face go red.

"BEES?!" George yelled; a laughter erupted,
"Those tiny little things?
No one likes bugs; they're creepy and small."
My ears began to ring.

"W..w...well," I had stuttered,
Swallowing down my fears.
"The different nectars make different honey."
The class had stopped their sneers.

"A lot of plants depend on bees,"
They started to see my affection.
"All worker bees are actually women,
They dance to show direction."

I stood up straight and spoke with pride.
I wanted to share my wisdom.
"Worker bees are pollinators,
They help our ecosystem."

"So, bees are actually smart?" George asked.
A smile grew on my face.
"They're more than smart, George," I explained
"They save the human race."

LITTLE BOY BLUE

Little boy blue,
Didn't always feel blue.
In fact, sometimes, he felt yellow.

"You stay over there in your little blue house!"
Even though he was blue,
He felt yellow.

Little boy blue didn't always feel blue.
But he was told to be blue when he wasn't.

He grew up to be blue.
They told him, "Be blue!"
Despite that, he knew!
In order to feel you,
He didn't be blue, he was yellow!

BEING ME

I care about me.
I am beautiful and kind.
Weird and wondrous.

Printed in Great Britain
by Amazon

66082654R00015